EPIC
EMPIRES

PHILIP STEELE

WAYLAND

CONTENTS

BRITISH EMPIRE

THE AZTECS

SPANISH EMPIRE

THE INCA LANDS

**ANCIENT
ROMANS**

**THE
MONGOLS**

THE OTTOMANS

ANCIENT PERSIA

**IMPERIAL
CHINA**

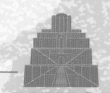

BABYLON

ANCIENT EGYPT

**EARLY INDIAN
EMPIRES**

INTRODUCTION

An empire usually covers a large area and is a group of states and peoples governed by a single ruler (the emperor or empress), or a small group of people.

Many empires have grown from a single city, expanding as the people take control of neighbouring regions, to cover huge areas stretching across continents. The development of ships that could cross oceans meant that distant territories on the other side of the world could be brought under control, creating empires that stretched right around the planet. These global empires became hubs for trade and industry, as goods and raw materials were shipped across thousands of kilometres of seas and oceans.

THE WORD 'EMPIRE' COMES FROM THE LATIN TERM 'IMPERIUM', MEANING POWER.

THE EMPIRE OF ALEXANDER THE GREAT WAS ONE OF THE WORLD'S LARGEST, BUT IT ONLY LASTED FOR EIGHT YEARS.

Many of the European empires of Africa and the Americas were known for their brutality. On his arrival in South America at the start of the 16th century, Hernán Cortés (above) oversaw the rapid conquest of the Aztecs and the beginnings of Spain's brutal regime in the region.

Different empires have also treated their subjects in different ways. Some have created fair laws and overseen periods of peace and stability that have led to great advances in science, technology, crafts and the arts. However, others have ruled with brutality, stripping their conquered lands of wealth, and enslaving or slaughtering the indigenous peoples.

At some point, nearly every part of the world has been ruled by an empire. Today, only a few remnants exist of empires that once circled the globe, but plenty of ruins and relics remain to remind us of the power of these once-mighty civilisations.

Completed by Emperor Hadrian in 128 CE, this wall in England (main image) marked the northern edge of the Roman empire. The wall was nearly 120 km (75 miles) long and stretched across Britain.

BABYLON
CITY OF TWO EMPIRES

Name:	First Babylonian empire
Dates:	1792–1595 BCE
Region:	Mesopotamia, between the rivers Tigris and Euphrates
Famous rulers:	Hammurabi

Name:	Second Babylonian empire
Dates:	626–539 BCE
Region:	Persian Gulf to the eastern Mediterranean Sea
Famous rulers:	Nebuchadnezzar II

From 2334 BCE, several cities in western Asia joined together to form the world's first empire, known as the Akkadian empire. One of these cities, Babylon, rose in power and, by 1792 BCE, it was ruling an empire in its own right.

Sitting on the east bank of the Euphrates, Babylon was one of the biggest cities in the world at the time. It had 1,179 temples and the walls protecting it from attack were 18 km (11 miles) long. One of its key buildings was an enormous stepped pyramid, called a ziggurat. It had seven storeys and may have been the source for the Bible story of the Tower of Babel. One of this empire's greatest rulers was Hammurabi, who defeated many neighbouring kingdoms and extended the empire.

1ST BABYLONIAN EMPIRE
2ND BABYLONIAN EMPIRE

Euphrates · Tigris · Persia · Mari · Mediterranean Sea · Jerusalem · Babylon · BABYLONIAN EMPIRE · Egypt · Ur · Persian Gulf · Red Sea · Arabia

CITY OF WONDERS

By the time Nebuchadnezzar II took control of the empire, Babylon was a major centre for trade along the Euphrates river. The city itself was laid out in a grid, with the largest road, known as the Processional Way, running in the same direction as the Euphrates. As well as temples, gates and gardens, the city had two huge palaces covering 16 hectares (39.5 acres).

AT ITS PEAK, BABYLON COVERED 10 SQ. KM (4 SQ. MILES).

KEY DATES

1792–1750 BCE

In 1792 BCE, Hammurabi becomes ruler of Babylon and turns it into an empire. In 1760 BCE, Hammurabi has the laws of Babylon carved on a pillar of stone.

More than a thousand years later, Babylon rose to power once again. One of its rulers, Nebuchadnezzar II, believed that Babylon was the centre of the universe. He rebuilt the ziggurat, as well as new city walls and canals. A processional way honoured the god Marduk. An old legend tells how the king built a beautiful terraced park for his wife, Amytis, but there is no proof that these 'Hanging Gardens' ever existed.

Towards the end of his reign, Hammurabi (shown standing on the left) drew up a set of laws for his people. These laws listed crimes and the punishments for them. He had the laws carved onto a large stone pillar, called a stela, so that everyone could see them.

At the north end of the Processional Way was the colourful Ishtar Gate. It was decorated with images of bulls (main image) and dragons. The road itself was made from burned bricks and stones that had been carefully shaped to fit together.

626–605 BCE

From 626 BCE, Babylon becomes powerful again under King Nabopolassar. In 605 BCE, his son Nebuchadnezzar II defeats the Egyptians and Assyrians at Carchemish.

605–539 BCE

In 586 BCE, Nebuchadnezzar II sacks Jerusalem. Many Jews are sent to Babylon in exile. In 539 BCE, the Persian king Cyrus the Great captures the city of Babylon.

ANCIENT EGYPT

Name:	Egypt's African empire
Dates:	c.1950–1650 BCE, c.1550–1069 BCE
Region:	Southwards into Nubia (modern Sudan)

Name:	Egypt's Asian empire
Dates:	c.1550–1069 BCE
Region:	modern Palestine, Lebanon, Syria
Famous rulers:	Thutmose I and Ramesses II

The ancient Egyptian civilisation grew up along the banks of the River Nile. The river provided water for drinking and irrigation, and fertile mud for the fields. Egypt grew wealthy and many of its great pyramids and temples survive today.

The Nile and the Red Sea also provided access to the African lands to the south. After about 3000 BCE, the Egyptians traded and mined in Nubia or Kush. From the 1900s BCE, they built forts, which helped them control the region and its borders for about 250 years. In 760 BCE, Nubian rulers came to power in Egypt itself.

AFRICAN EMPIRE

ASIAN EMPIRE

EGYPT WAS ABSORBED INTO THE PERSIAN EMPIRE IN 525 BCE.

c.3000–1650 BCE

The Egyptians start pushing southwards into Nubia (Sudan), trading and mining as they go. In the 1900s and 1800s BCE, they build forts in Nubia and mark out borders. They lose control of the region in about 1650 BCE.

1550–1457 BCE

The pharaoh Thutmose I attacks the Mitanni State in northern Syria. His son Thutmose II regains control of Nubia. At the battle and long siege of Megiddo in about 1457 BCE,

The period from 1550–1070 BCE is known as the New Kingdom. A string of rulers, including Thutmose I and Ramesses II, reunited the African part of the empire and invaded the Middle East, battling against the Mitanni State, the Hittites and the Sea Peoples who were living in Palestine and Syria at the time. The period was marked by the construction of many large buildings, such as the temples at Karnak and Luxor, and the tombs in the Valley of the Kings.

Ramesses II fought the Hittites in the Battle of Qadesh in 1274 BCE (above). It was seen as a victory over the Hittites, but neither side won outright. In 1259 BCE, the pharaoh signed a peace treaty with the Hittite king, Hattusilis III.

ARMIES

Egypt's new empire builders relied on their armies. War chariots were introduced into Egypt in the 1500s BCE. The khopesh was a curved bronze weapon, that was used like a sword. Footsoldiers were armed with shields and spears, while the most effective weapons were bows and arrows. By the 1200s BCE, leather armour with metal scales was being worn.

1279–1069 BCE

Thutmose III defeats rulers from Syria and Palestine.

In about 1274 BCE, Ramesses II takes on the powerful Hittite empire, fighting a great battle at Qadesh in Syria. Ramesses III defeats the Libyans and the Sea Peoples. By 1069 BCE, Egypt has lost both Asia and Nubia.

Ramesses II built this huge temple (main image) at Abu Simbel in Nubia. The four towering figures guarding the entrance to the temple are 20 m (65 ft) tall and represent the Egyptian pharaoh.

ANCIENT PERSIA

Name:	The Achaemenid empire
Dates:	c.552–330 BCE
Region:	From Egypt to India, the Black Sea to Central Asia
Famous rulers:	Cyrus (Kurash) II (the Great), Darius (Daryavaush) I, Xerxes (Khshayarsha) I

The first Persian empire was the greatest the ancient world had seen, covering about 8 million square km (5 million sq miles) of Asia, Africa and Europe. It defeated Babylon in 539 BCE.

Under the leadership of Cyrus II (the Great), the Persian empire pushed east towards the Indus river and west into Greece.

The lands of the empire were divided into provinces called satrapies, with governors called satraps. Each province paid tributes to the 'king of kings'. The rulers believed in one god, called Ahura-Mazda. They built fine palaces and cities such as Persepolis (Parsa, c.518 BCE), a royal road and irrigation schemes. Cyrus's successor, Darius I, issued gold coins, which were used across the empire and beyond.

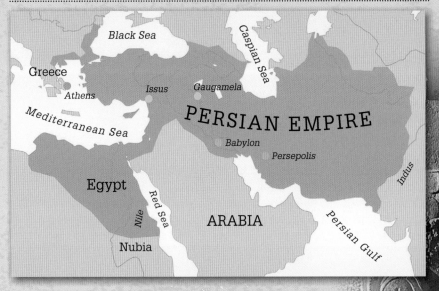

INNOVATIONS

The Persians are credited with developing many innovations. These include the standardisation of weights, money and measurements across the region, new standards of metalworking, building, arts and crafts, an imperial postal service, and a system of regional government which allowed them to control such a huge area.

XERXES INVADED GREECE WITH

KEY DATES

552–499 BCE

The Persian king Cyrus II of Anshan overthrows the Medes and establishes a new empire. The empire grows rapidly, taking in Babylon, the Indus Valley and eventually Egypt. Persepolis becomes the new capital.

499–479 BCE

In 499 BCE, Greeks under Persian rule revolt, starting a long war between Persia and Greece. In 480 BCE, the Persians sack Athens. By 479 BCE, the Persians have been forced to give up their plans for conquering Greece.

Wars broke out between Persia and Greek city states from 499 to 449 BCE. The then Persian ruler Xerxes assembled a huge army and fleet which contained 47 different nationalities, but even they could not conquer the Greeks.

In 334 BCE, Alexander II of Macedon (also known as Alexander the Great) invaded the Persian empire with a Greek army. He was a brilliant soldier and defeated Darius III, ending the Persian empire. It was not until 227 CE that a new Persian empire arose, ruled by the Sassanid kings.

Coins issued by Darius I, such as this one, have been found at archaeological sites in Greece, Macedonia and as far west as Italy, showing how far the influence of the Persian empire stretched.

130,000 SOLDIERS.

334–330 BCE

Alexander the Great invades the Persian empire. He defeats Darius III at Issus in 333 BCE. In 331 BCE, Alexander wins at Gaugamela. Darius III dies in 330 BCE and the empire falls.

Alexander the Great destroyed the city of Persepolis (main image) in 330 BCE. He needed 20,000 mules and 5,000 camels to carry away all the treasure that was kept there.

EARLY INDIAN EMPIRES

INDIA'S GOLDEN AGE

India's first large empires brought about a great age of literature, art, science and religious expression.

Name:	The Mauryan empire
Dates:	322–185 BCE
Region:	Most of what is now India, Pakistan and Afghanistan
Famous rulers:	Chandragupta Maurya, Ashoka

Name:	The Gupta empire
Dates:	320–550 CE
Region:	Northern and eastern India
Famous rulers:	Chandragupta I, II, Samudragupta

The Mauryan empire, founded in 322 BCE, ruled from its capital at Pataliputra (modern Patna). It was well governed and recaptured lands in the northwest that had been taken by Alexander the Great (see page 11). Under the rule of Ashoka, the empire pushed to its greatest extent, conquering neighbouring realms, such as Kalinga to the east. At the time, it was one of the largest empires in the world.

MAURYAN EMPIRE

GUPTA EMPIRE

Himalayas

Patalla

Pataliputra

Sanchi

Indian Ocean

The peace and stability of the Gupta empire allowed the people to develop many trades, arts and crafts. They were highly prized as silk weavers, iron workers, potters and jewellers.

According to some accounts, 100,000 people were killed during the war with Kalinga. Ashoka was so appalled by this destruction that he converted to Buddhism. As a result, the religion spread throughout the empire, as seen by Buddhist temples from the period (left).

KEY DATES

322–232 BCE

In 322 BCE, Chandragupta Maurya seizes control of Meghada, founding the Mauryan empire. His son Bindusara pushes south from 298 BCE.

Five centuries later, the powerful Gupta empire enjoyed a long period of peace and prosperity. The empire stretched across the northern half of the Indian subcontinent and featured many great advances in science, literature, architecture and mathematics.

Towards the end of the fifth century CE, nomadic peoples from the northwest, called the Huns, started to invade Gupta territory. The empire began to decline and break up into smaller states.

THE MAURYAN EMPIRE RULED MORE THAN 50 MILLION PEOPLE.

SCIENCE AND RELIGION

Chandragupta Maurya followed the Jain religion, which believes that all forms of life are sacred. Ashoka became a Buddhist, while the Gupta rulers were devout Hindus, building many temples throughout the empire (main image). India saw a golden age of philosophy, yoga, astronomy, poetry and sculpture. Indian mathematicians brought in the numerical system with a zero, which we still use today.

232 BCE–320 CE

From 272 BCE, Ashoka rules the biggest ever Indian empire.

In the years after Ashoka's death, the Mauryan empire goes into decline, breaking up in 185 BCE. In 320 CE, a new Gupta empire is founded by the Hindu king Chandragupta I.

320–550 CE

Gupta rule extends over a large part of northern India. From the 480s CE onwards, invaders break through in the northwest and the Gupta rulers lose their grip over the region.

IMPERIAL CHINA

BEHIND THE GREAT WALL

Name:	The Chinese empire
Dates:	221 BCE–1911 CE
Region:	Variable, spreading outwards from eastern regions up to and sometimes beyond today's borders
Famous rulers:	Qin Shi Huang, Tai Zong of Tang, Empress Wu Zeitian, Taizu of Song, Kublai Khan, Chengzu of Ming, Kangxi emperor, Qianlong emperor

The Chinese empire saw two thousand years of civilisation, interrupted only by occasional periods of disunity or invasion.

For hundreds of years, the Chinese region had many different states that regularly fought each other. One state, Qin, started to defeat the other territories. By 221 BCE, it had united all the states to form a single empire. Its king, Zheng, took the title of 'First Sovereign Emperor' or Qin Shi Huang.

Over the ages different dynasties or royal families ruled China. They included the Han, Tang, Ming and Qing.

When the first Chinese emperor, Qin Shi Huang, died in 210 BCE, his tomb was guarded by a whole army of life-sized statues. Since the site was uncovered in 1974, nearly 8,000 figures in this terracotta army have been found.

THE QING DYNASTY RULED 432 MILLION PEOPLE – ABOUT 35 PER CENT OF THE WORLD'S POPULATION AT THE TIME.

KEY DATES

221 BCE–700s CE

In 221 BCE, China unites as an empire under Qin Shi Huang. Many other dynasties rise and fall over the centuries. From 585 CE, a Grand Canal is built, north to south. The 700s CE are an age of classic art and literature.

700s–1644

1215 marks the start of Mongol invasions. They found the Yuan dynasty in 1279. The Ming dynasty starts in 1368, and is best known for its fine porcelain and voyages of exploration.

The Great Wall served as a route for messengers and traders, but its defences could not keep out Mongol invaders in the 13th century. They ruled as the Yuan dynasty and adopted Chinese ways. Their capital was Cambaluc (Beijing).

Each period of dynastic rule saw great changes in how China dealt with the outside world. Some periods were marked by extensive trade and exploration, while others saw the empire close its doors to the outside world. Having reached its peak during the Qing dynasty, which had ruled since 1644, Imperial China was finally overthrown by nationalists in 1911.

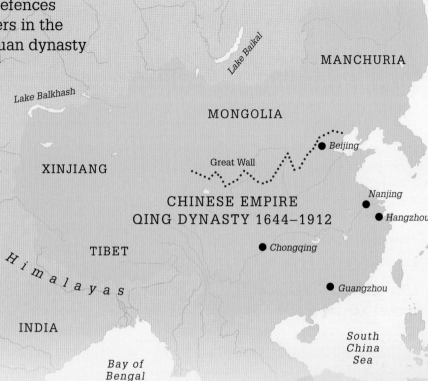

Lake Baikal

MANCHURIA

Lake Balkhash

MONGOLIA

XINJIANG

● Beijing

Great Wall

CHINESE EMPIRE
QING DYNASTY 1644–1912

● Nanjing

● Hangzhou

TIBET

● Chongqing

Himalayas

● Guangzhou

INDIA

South China Sea

Bay of Bengal

The Great Wall (main image) was built across northern China over a period of 2,000 years. Its main course was 2,400 km (1,500 miles) long, but all the defences may have totalled more than 21,000 km (13,000 miles).

1644–1911

In 1644, Manchus from northeast found the last dynasty, the Qing. In the 1800s, European powers seize territory. After a series of uprisings, the last emperor, a boy called Puyi, is overthrown by nationalist leader Sun Yatsen.

GUNPOWDER

The Chinese invented gunpowder around the 800s CE. They used this explosive black powder in various weapons, such as rockets and grenades, and later in guns and cannons. The Mongols took gunpowder weapons with them when they marched westwards, introducing them to Europeans in the 13th century.

ANCIENT ROMANS

ALL ROADS LEAD TO ROME

Name:	The Roman empire
Dates:	27 BCE–476 CE
Region:	North to Britain, south to Africa, west to Spain and east into Asia
Famous rulers:	Augustus, Tiberius, Caligula, Claudius, Nero, Vespasian, Titus, Domitian, Trajan, Hadrian, Marcus Aurelius, Diocletian, Constantine I

In 507 BCE, the city of Rome overthrew its king and became a republic. Over the next 500 years, it expanded, pushing its borders far beyond the city to take control of Italy, Spain, France and North Africa.

However, a series of civil wars weakened the republic and, in 27 BCE, Augustus Caesar seized control as sole ruler. He transformed the republic into an empire.

Under the rule of Augustus, the empire continued to expand, conquering lands as far away as northern Britain, southwards to include Egypt and North Africa, and eastwards to Babylonia and the mouth of the Euphrates. Leading this expansion was the Roman army, a very effective military force. The army conquered any territory that failed to surrender freely to Roman rule.

CONSTRUCTION

The impressive ruins of the Roman empire can still be seen, from the Pont du Gard in southern France (main image) to Gerasa (Jerash) in Jordan. The Romans were masters of brick and concrete, building great arches and domes. They built houses and palaces with underfloor heating and piped water.

KEY DATES

250 BCE–27 CE

By about 250 BCE, Rome controls Italy. By 146 BCE, it rules Greece, and by 31 BCE it governs Egypt and North Africa. In 27 CE, Rome becomes an empire, under the rule of Augustus.

For its first 200 years, the empire enjoyed a period of peace and prosperity. This period is known as *Pax Romana* ('Roman Peace'). Roman armies controlled huge areas of land and built roads and forts. Roman slaves worked in the mines, its gladiators fought in the arena, and its merchants travelled far and wide.

After this period, invasions, civil wars and other threats destabilised the empire, causing it to split in two – the western empire ruled from Rome and the eastern Byzantine empire ruled from Constantinople (Istanbul).

The emperor Trajan was a successful military leader who expanded the empire to its greatest size by the time of his death in 117 CE. Trajan's Column in Rome (right) was built to commemorate his military campaign against the Dacians, who lived where Romania is today. This campaign pushed the boundaries of the empire beyond the Danube river.

THE EMPIRE COVERED TERRITORIES IN 40 MODERN COUNTRIES.

At its peak, the empire covered an area of 6.5 million sq km (2.5 million sq miles) – almost the size of the whole of Australia. It governed an estimated population of between 70–100 million people.

27–117 CE

In 79 CE, the volcano Vesuvius erupts, burying the towns of Pompeii and Herculaneum. When Trajan dies in 117 CE, the Roman empire has reached its greatest extent.

117–476 CE

In 330 CE, Constantinople (Istanbul) becomes the eastern capital. In 476 CE, Rome and the empire in the west collapses, while the eastern or Byzantine empire continues until 1453 CE.

THE MONGOLS

STORM OUT OF THE EAST

Name:	The Mongol empire
Dates:	1206–1368
Region:	From the Pacific Ocean to Eastern Europe
Famous rulers:	Genghis Khan, Kublai Khan

For centuries, peoples living in the grasslands and deserts of central and eastern Asia had led a nomadic life, moving from pasture to pasture and raiding rich lands to the south and west.

That changed in the 13th century, when these nomads joined together to create a powerful military force that conquered a huge area of land, creating the largest continuous empire the world has ever seen.

MONGOL

Black Sea

Caspian Sea

Kashgar ●

SYRIA

Mediterranean Sea

P E R S I A

Baghdad ●

● Kerman

A R A B I A

Himalayas

I N D I A

Arabian Sea

A MONGOL ARMY WAS ABLE TO COVER 160 KM (100 MILES) A DAY ON HORSEBACK.

KEY DATES

1206–1229

In 1206, Mongols unite under Genghis Khan. They attack parts of China and invade Central Asia from 1218. In 1223, the Mongols attack the East Slavs. Genghis Khan dies in 1227 and is succeeded by his son Ögedai in 1229.

Mongol warriors were excellent horse riders, and each rider kept two or three horses in reserve. The extra horses meant they could cover huge amounts of ground. They were also very skilled with the bow and arrow.

The Mongols united under the leadership of a warrior called Temujin, whom they named Genghis Khan, meaning 'lord of all'. His armies swept into China, Central Asia, Persia and Russia and by the time of his death in 1227, the Mongols ruled an area that was twice the size of the Roman empire. Ögedai, Genghis's son, pushed the empire's boundaries even further into China, Korea and eastern Europe. Genghis's grandsons then divided the huge empire between them, with Kublai Khan founding the Yuan dynasty, which ruled China (see page 15).

Having reached its maximum size, the empire was weakened by a series of quarrels about successions and civil wars. The Mongols lost China in 1368, with Persia falling not long after.

NOMADS

The Mongols never really forgot their origins as nomads, moving from one pasture to another. They were fierce fighters and were widely feared, but the states they founded were often very civilised. By 1368, their empire was falling apart, although other Mongol and Turkic peoples created later empires.

MONGOLIA

EMPIRE

Shangdu ●
● Cambaluc (Beijing)

KOREA

● Lanzhou

CHINA

Pacific Ocean

● Yunnan

South China Sea

The power and mobility of the Mongol army is celebrated in this huge statue of Genghis Khan on horseback (main image). It is 40 m (130 ft) tall and stands just outside the Mongolian capital of Ulaanbaatar.

1230–1260

Mongol hordes swarm into China, Korea, Russia, Georgia, Armenia and Eastern and Central Europe. In the 1250s, they invade Vietnam, destroy Baghdad and invade Syria.

1260–1368

By 1279, Kublai Khan controls all China. He dies in 1294. Mongol rule ends in China in 1368. The Mongol states fragment, although a later empire is created by Timur towards the end of the 1300s.

THE OTTOMANS

Name:	The Ottoman empire
Dates:	1299–1923
Region:	From southeast Europe to Western Asia and North Africa
Famous rulers:	Osman I, Mehmet II, Suleiman the Magnificent

Like the Mongols, groups of Turkic peoples had come out of Asia in the Middle Ages, hungry for land, power and wealth. The Oghuz Turks were Muslims, who from 1299 were ruled by the Ottoman dynasty.

EUROPE

Vienna
Venice
Belgrade
Sofia
Sevastopol
Black Sea
Istanbul
Athens
Algiers
Tunis
Mediterranean Sea
Tripoli
Damascus
Baghdad
Jerusalem
Cairo
ARABIA
AFRICA

In 1453, under the leadership of Mehmet II, the Ottomans defeated the Byzantine empire (see page 17) by capturing its capital, Constantinople, which they called Istanbul. The empire continued to expand in all directions.

Suleiman the Magnificent (left on horseback) was an excellent military leader. During his rule, the empire conquered Rhodes and Belgrade, most of Hungary and large parts of the Middle East. He also pushed across North Africa as far as modern Algeria.

KEY DATES

1299–1453

In 1299, Osman I founds the Ottoman empire. During the 1300s, it conquers Serbia and Bulgaria. In 1453, Mehmet II captures Constantinople (Istanbul), capital of the Byzantine empire.

From 1520, under the reign of Suleiman the Magnificent, the Ottoman empire was at its peak. It eventually took in southeast Europe, Egypt and North Africa, Palestine, Syria and Iraq. In 1529, Suleiman the Magnificent laid siege to Vienna, but failed to take the city. The Ottomans tried once more in 1683, but again they were beaten back.

After this followed a period of stagnation and decline until the 20th century and World War I, when the empire entered the conflict in support of Germany. After the defeat, the empire was broken up by the victorious Allied powers.

AT ITS PEAK, THE EMPIRE STRETCHED OVER THREE CONTINENTS.

After the fall of Constantinople, the Ottoman rulers transformed the city. They built a beautiful royal residence, known as the Topkapi Palace, and changed the Christian basilica into a huge mosque, known as Hagia Sophia (main image).

1453–1683

The empire reaches its peak under Suleiman I ('the Magnificent'). In 1529, he besieges Vienna. In 1571, Spain and Venice check Ottoman naval power at Lepanto. In 1683, the Ottomans are defeated on land at Vienna.

1683–1923

The empire goes into decline and territories are lost. Greece fights for independence 1821–1832. In 1914, the Ottomans join with Germany and Austria in World War I, and are defeated in 1918.

THE AZTECS

Name:	The Aztec empire
Dates:	1325–1521
Region:	Central Mexico and parts of Central America
Famous rulers:	Moctezuma I, Ahuitzol, Moctezuma II

Having been a nomadic people for more than 200 years, the Aztecs settled in central Mexico and created a powerful but brutal empire.

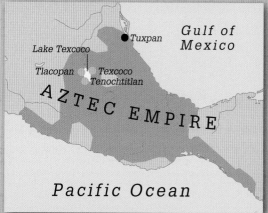

In about 1100, the Aztecs left their homeland in northern Mexico. After many years of wandering and hardship, they saw an eagle with a snake in its claws land on a cactus on an island in the middle of Lake Texcoco. They believed that this was a sign from their god they should settle in the area permanently.

In 1325, they built a new city called Tenochtitlan that became their capital. It was an amazing city of squares, temple-pyramids, palaces, schools, markets, ball courts and floating gardens.

In 1519, Spanish soldiers landed in Mexico. They rode horses (left) and were armed with deadly iron swords and guns. Within two years and with the help of the Aztecs' local enemies, they had destroyed Tenochtitlan and ended the Aztec empire.

KEY DATES

1195–1428

In about 1195, the Aztecs arrive in the Valley of Mexico and Tenochtitlan is built in 1325. In 1428, the cities of Tenochtitlan, Texcoco and Tlacopan join to form the empire.

At its peak, Tenochtitlan covered nearly 15 sq km (6 sq miles) and was home to 250,000 people. This city joined with two others, Texcoco and Tlacopan, to form a Triple Alliance, which ruled an empire. The empire grew quickly, conquering neighbouring lands until it controlled nearly all of central Mexico. Despite its strength, however, it was poorly equipped to face invaders from the east and it quickly crumbled when Europeans first appeared.

ELITE FIGHTERS

Aztec armies fought with shields, spears and clubs. Swords were strips of wood lined with a razor-sharp, glassy stone called obsidian. Elite warriors joined a specific fighting group, such as the Eagles or the Jaguars. In combat, warriors would often try to capture opponents rather than kill them. These captives could then be sacrificed to appease the gods.

THE SYMBOL OF THE EAGLE ON A CACTUS IS ON THE MEXICAN FLAG.

The Aztecs practised human sacrifice where the hearts of the victims were cut out. It was believed to be a great honour to die in this way. Some estimates say that as many as 20,000 people were sacrificed every year.

1429–1519

Ahuitzol becomes ruler and is followed by Moctezuma II in 1502. The Aztec empire is at its greatest. In 1519, Spanish soldiers led by Hernán Cortés arrive in ships and they capture Moctezuma.

1520–1523

The Spanish are forced to flee but return, destroying the city after a long siege. In 1523, Mexico City is built on the same site, and Mexico becomes a colony of the Spanish empire.

THE INCA LANDS

EMPIRE OF THE SUN

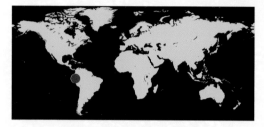

Name:	The Inca empire
Dates:	c.1100–1536
Region:	The Andes mountains and coastal plains, from northern Chile through Peru northwards towards Ecuador
Famous rulers:	Pachacuti Inca Yupanqui, Wayna Qapaq

The Inca empire was the last of many great civilisations that had developed since 1000 BCE in the thin strip of land between the Andes and the Pacific coast in South America.

At the centre of the empire was the capital of Cuzco, which was founded in 1100 CE. In the years that followed, the Incas formed alliances with their neighbours and expanded their territory. From about 1300, their leaders claimed the title *Sapa Inca*, meaning 'the only Inca', and traced their ancestry back to the Sun god to justify their claim to rule. One of these rulers, Pachacuti Inca Yupanqui, transformed the Cuzco kingdom into an enormous empire from 1438.

Quito
Cajamarca
Machu Picchu
Lima
Cuzco
Andes
Lake Titicaca
Pacific Ocean
Andes

INCA ACCOUNTING

The Incas used knotted strings called 'quipu' to keep records and make calculations. Each quipu was made up of a long rope with several strings hanging from it. Knots were tied in these strings to represent units, tens and hundreds of whatever was being counted. The strings could also be colour-coded to represent different subjects, such as tribute or lands.

THE INCAS RULED OVER 12 MILLION PEOPLE.

KEY DATES

c.1100–1492

Cuzco is founded in 1100. By 1437, the Inca empire is growing rapidly. From 1471, roads are built across the empire, and by 1492, the Inca empire stretches south to Chile.

The Inca ruler Pachacuti (right), carried out a series of conquests that expanded the Inca empire up and down the South American continent to its maximum size. He ruled until 1471, when he died following an illness.

VPANQVI

Reyno has ta chile y de to onsucor selloca

At its peak, the empire measured just 320 km (200 miles) from east to west, but it stretched north to south for about 3,600 km (2,250 miles). Linking the towns and villages were roads and bridges that spanned mountain passes and coastal plains. The Incas were master builders and they cut stones so carefully that they could create buildings strong enough to survive the region's earthquakes. They also built irrigation channels and turned the mountain slopes into terraced fields to grow crops such as potatoes, quinoa and maize.

Spanish troops, led by Francesco Pisarro, arrived in the region in 1532 and the Inca empire soon collapsed. Even so, a few Inca cities, such as Machu Picchu (main image), survived in remote mountainous places.

1493–1532

In 1493, Wayna Qapaq becomes emperor. In 1498, he pushes north into Colombia. After his death there is civil war. In 1532, Atahualpa becomes emperor and Francesco Pisarro invades with Spanish troops.

1532–1572

Atahualpa is taken prisoner. After a vast ransom is raised by the Incas, he is murdered and Cuzco is destroyed in 1536. The empire falls, but the Incas resist Spanish rule until 1572.

SPANISH EMPIRE

INTO THE NEW WORLD

Name:	The Spanish empire
Dates:	1402–1975
Region:	Parts of Europe, Africa, North and South America, Asia and Oceania
Famous rulers:	The Catholic Monarchs (Ferdinand and Isabella), Emperor Charles V, King Philip II

Spain and Portugal were the first countries to truly explore the whole globe. In 1492, Christopher Columbus, an Italian in the service of Spain, sailed west and discovered the Americas.

This 'New World' was looted, enslaved and settled. Spain's territories spread into Mexico, California and across South America, with Brazil taken by Portugal. Treasure ships carried vast amounts of silver, gold and emeralds back to Europe. By 1521, Ferdinand Magellan's voyage into the Pacific Ocean had even brought the Philippines under Spanish rule. The Spanish conquerors were driven by the desire for land, riches and power, and to spread the Christian faith.

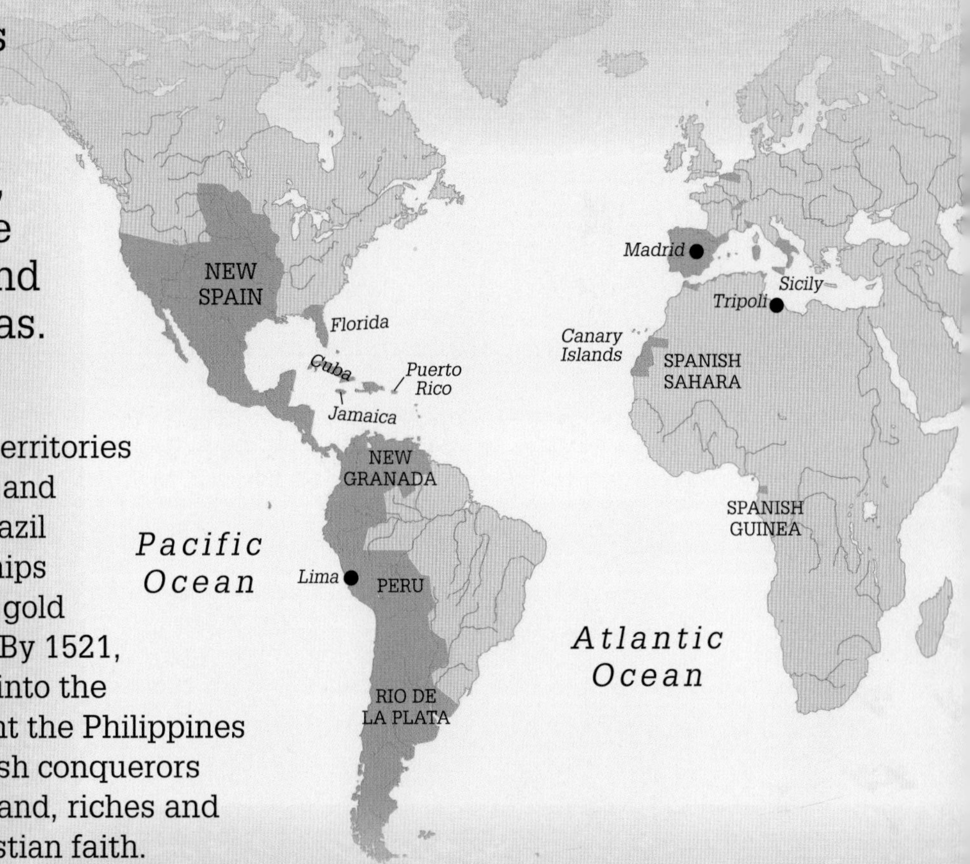

Map labels: NEW SPAIN · Florida · Cuba · Puerto Rico · Jamaica · NEW GRANADA · Pacific Ocean · Lima · PERU · RIO DE LA PLATA · Atlantic Ocean · Madrid · Sicily · Tripoli · Canary Islands · SPANISH SAHARA · SPANISH GUINEA

TODAY, 405 MILLION PEOPLE SPEAK SPANISH IN 47 DIFFERENT COUNTRIES.

KEY DATES

1402–1503

In 1402, the conquest of the Canary Islands marks the start of a Spanish empire. Between 1492–1503, Columbus makes four voyages to the New World and the colonisation of the Americas begins.

1504–1600s

In the 1500s, the Spanish extend their rule into North and South America and the Philippines. Emperor Charles V (1500–1558) rules large areas of Europe as well as the Americas.

This coin (left) is a Spanish 8 reales from the reign of Philip IV (1621–1665). It was made in Mexico City and was used throughout the Spanish empire. It became known as a 'piece of eight'. To begin with, the coin was made by cutting off the right amount of silver from a large bar, flattening it into an irregular shape and then stamping it with an official hammer.

This wealth made Spain the most powerful country in Europe. It also made it a target for other countries who wanted to take this wealth, and Spanish treasure fleets were attacked by ships from rival nations and by pirates.

The empire started to weaken with competition from rising European powers, such as the Netherlands and Britain. Pressure in North America during the 18th century reduced Spanish influence there and uprisings throughout South America in the 19th century created new independent nations.

SILVER HORDE

Between 1556 and 1783, some 41,000 tonnes of silver were extracted from the mines of Potosí in Bolivia alone. The crown was entitled to one-fifth of all the gold and silver mined in the colonies and about 8,200 tonnes of the silver mined at Potosí were sent back to the Spanish royal family.

Manilla ● PHILIPPINES

1700s–1899

Increasing competition from rival nations and wars in Europe see a decline of the empire's power. Latin American possessions break away throughout the 1800s.

Part of the legacy of the Spanish empire is the architecture that can be found throughout its territories. These include ornate palaces, government buildings and churches, such as this one in Lima, Peru (main image).

BRITISH EMPIRE

Name:	The British empire
Dates:	1583–1997
Region:	parts of Europe, Africa, North and South America, Asia and Oceania
Famous rulers:	Elizabeth I, George III, Victoria

Envious of the Spanish and Portuguese empires of the 16th and 17th centuries, the British started to claim foreign territories. Over a period of 400 years, they created the largest empire the world has ever seen.

From the 1580s, Britain started to explore, establish colonies and set up international trading companies. Its power spread around the globe, from North America and the Caribbean to India, Africa and eventually Australia and New Zealand.

In 1775–1783, Britain's North American colonies fought for their independence before breaking away to form the USA.

TRADE

Trade was a key factor in pushing the expansion of the British empire. From India to southern China, the driving force behind this trade was the East India Company, whose ships carried valuable goods back to Britain (main image). It worked closely with the British government and navy to protect British interests in the area throughout the 19th century.

KEY DATES

1583–1783

In 1583, Newfoundland is claimed for Britain and Virginia is settled from 1607. The North American colonies revolt and win their independence in 1783.

1783–1947

Slavery is abolished in the British empire in 1833. The empire spreads across the globe, and reaches its greatest size just after World War I. However, there are growing calls for independence.

CANADA
13 COLONIES
Atlantic Ocean
Pacific Ocean
Jamaica
BRITISH GUIANA
GREAT BRITAIN
IRELAND
Cyprus
IRAQ
EGYPT
NIGERIA   SUDAN
SOUTH AFRICA
INDIA
BURMA
Hong Kong
Singapore
MALAYA
Indian Ocean
AUSTRALIA
PAPUA NEW GUINEA
NEW ZEALAND

AT ITS PEAK, THE BRITISH EMPIRE COVERED ONE-QUARTER OF EARTH'S LAND AREA.

Following the end of World War II, the British empire shrank very quickly. From 1945 to 1965, the number of people outside the UK who were under British rule fell from 400 million to just 5 million.

During the reign of Queen Victoria, Britain's global empire was held together by naval and military power, by railways and steam ships, by the newly invented telegraph, and by commerce. Following the expense of two world wars, however, the empire was greatly weakened, and many countries became independent during this period. Today, many of the countries that were part of the empire have joined together to create the Commonwealth of Nations to promote democracy and individual liberty.

Queen Victoria was the longest serving British monarch, reigning for 63 years and seven months from 24 May 1819 until her death on 22 January 1901. She was made Empress of India in 1877. During her reign, the British empire reached the peak of its power and wealth, although it didn't reach its greatest size until just after World War I.

1947–1997

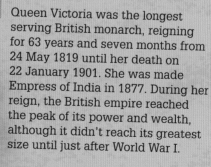

In the decades after World War II, most former British colonies become independent countries. In 1997, the British colony of Hong Kong is returned to China.

HALL OF FAME

AKKADIAN

Formed during the third millenium BCE, the Akkadian empire ruled an area of Mesopotamia from its capital city Akkad. Its greatest ruler was Sargon, who ruled the empire from about 2334–2279 BCE.

HITTITE

The Hittites formed one of the largest empires of the Middle East between 1400–1200 BCE. It stretched across what is now Turkey, northwest Syria and northern Iraq. The empire collapsed following squabbles over the throne, civil wars and invasions from outside enemies.

BYZANTINE

The eastern portion of the Roman empire, which came into existence in 285 CE and lasted until the fall of its capital city, Constantinople, in 1453. At its height, the empire stretched from Spain across to the Middle East.

UMAYYAD CALIPHATE

This was the fourth of the Islamic Caliphates (an Islamic state governed by a religious leader) established after the death of Muhammad. It lasted from 661–750 CE, and governed an area stretching from Spain to India, from its capital city of Damascus.

HOLY ROMAN EMPIRE

A large empire that ruled over central Europe for more than 1,000 years from the crowning of its first emperor, Charlemagne, in 800 CE. It was ruled by Frankish and German kings before eventually being dissolved in 1806 by its then emperor Francis II following defeat to Napoleon Bonaparte at the Battle of Austerlitz.

KHMER

This powerful empire ruled over a large area of Southeast Asia, including parts of modern-day Laos, Thailand and Vietnam. Governed from its capital city of Angkor, it lasted from 802 CE until the 1400s.

SONGHAI

Rising from the collapse of the Mali empire in the 1400s, Songhai expanded to govern a large area of northern Africa around the Niger River. It lasted for nearly 200 years, when it was defeated by an invading Moroccan army, who were keen to control the region's lucrative trade in gold.

FRENCH COLONIAL

France had two colonial periods. The first ended in 1814, with the defeat of Napoleon Bonaparte. The second started in the 1830s with conquests in Africa, Southeast Asia and the Pacific Ocean. In the 1920s and 1930s, the country ruled the second largest empire in the world, after the British.

DUTCH COLONIAL

Renowned for their skills in exploration, shipping and trade, the Dutch created an empire in parts of the Caribbean, South America, southern Africa and Southeast Asia.

RUSSIAN EMPIRE

Stretching from the Baltic Sea to the Pacific Ocean, the Russian empire was created in 1721 under the leadership of Tsar Peter the Great. Further expansion occurred under subsequent rulers, such as Catherine the Great and Alexander I, until the empire collapsed in 1917.

GLOSSARY

BASILICA
An important Roman Catholic church that has been given special rights by the Pope. Basilicas are usually pilgrimage sites and many people visit them every year.

CALLIGRAPHY
The art of writing beautiful words and letters. The writing is usually done with a brush or a pen with a specially shaped tip or nib.

CIVIL WAR
A war fought between two sides from the same country or region.

DYNASTY
A succession of rulers that come from the same family.

ENSLAVED
When people are captured and forced to work for others against their will, for no wages.

GLADIATOR
A person who fights other people or animals for the entertainment of a crowd.

IRRIGATION
Carrying water using a system of pipes and channels so that crops can be watered artificially.

LOOTED
When property and belongings are taken using force.

MINARET
A tall, thin tower that features a cone or onion-shaped top. Minarets are usually associated with mosques.

NOMAD
A person who does not live in one place and wanders from one spot to another in search of food or grazing for animals.

OBSIDIAN
A glass-like rock that is made from cooled lava. It can be broken to produce very sharp edges and has been used to make knives, swords and axes.

PASTURE
Land that is used for grazing by domesticated animals, such as horses and cattle.

PHARAOH
The term used to describe the ruler of ancient Egypt.

REPUBLIC
A country that is ruled by the people, not by a monarch.

SATRAPIES
The term used to describe the various regions of the ancient Persian empire. Each was overseen by a governor, called a satrap, who ruled on behalf of the emperor.

STELA (OR STELE)
A large slab made out of wood or stone. It is used to mark a boundary or to display official notices.

SUCCESSION
The replacement of a ruler by his or her successor.

TERRACOTTA
Clay that has been baked until it is hard.

TRIBUTE
A payment made by one party to another as a sign of respect or allegiance.

ZIGGURAT
A tall ceremonial building built in a series of layers that decrease in size, creating a stepped pyramid effect.

INDEX

First published in 2015 by Wayland

Copyright © Wayland 2015

Wayland
338 Euston Road
London NW1 3BH

Wayland Australia
Level 17/207 Kent Street
Sydney NSW 2000

All rights reserved.
Series editor: Elizabeth Brent

Produced by Tall Tree Ltd
Editor: Jon Richards
Designers: Ed Simkins and Jonathan Vipond

Dewey classification: 321'.03'09-dc23

ISBN: 978 0 7502 8755 5
ebook: 978 0 7502 8756 2
Printed in Malaysia

Wayland is a division of Hachette
Children's Books, an Hachette UK company.
www.hachette.co.uk

10 9 8 7 6 5 4 3 2 1

Picture credits
Front cover top Shutterstock/R-O-M-A, Front cover
bl Shutterstock/Yuri Yavnik, Front cover bc
Shutterstock, Front cover br Shutterstock/Bertl123,
1, 14-15 Shutterstock/fotohunter, 4-5 Shutterstock/
Ian McDonald, 5t Radiokul, 7t Mbzt/Creative
Commons Attribution 3.0 Unported license, 7b
Shutterstock/360b, 8-9 Shutterstock/Waj, 9t Stefano
Bianchetti/Corbis , 11t Deflim, 11b DEA/W. Buss/De
Agostini/Getty Images, 12bl Shutterstock/f9photos,
13 Shutterstock/JeremyRichards, 14cr Shutterstock/
Bule Sky Studio, 17t Shutterstock/Lucian Milasan,
17b Shutterstock/Bertl123, 18bl Yaan, 19
Shutterstock/hecke61, 20bl Wetwassermann, 20-21
Shutterstock/Mehmet Cetin, 22bl Tillman, 22-23
DEA/G. DAGLI ORTI/Getty, 24-25 Shutterstock/
Martchan, 25t Roarjo, 27tl OgreBot/Creative
Commons Attribution 3.0 Unported license, 27b
Shutterstock/Christian Vinces, 28-29 Heritage
Images/Corbis, 29br Quibik

GET EPIC!

Cross the globe on a journey of discovery and learn about some of the greatest events from the natural and human world. Read about the most epic migrations, battles, empires and explorers the world has ever seen.

9780750287579

9780750287616

9780750287555

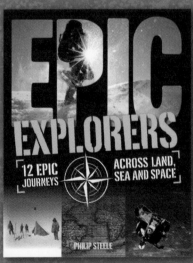

9780750287593